glitz it up

To Mum, Dad and Marc

THIS IS A CARLTON BOOK

Text, design and special photography copyright
© 2001 Carlton Books Limited

This edition published by Carlton Books Limited 2002
20 Mortimer Street, London W1T 3JW

A CIP catalogue record for this book is available from
the British Library
ISBN 1 84222 641 X

Printed and bound in Italy

Editorial Manager: Venetia Penfold
Art Director: Penny Stock
Executive Editor: Zia Mattocks
Senior Art Editor: Barbara Zuñiga
Writer/Editor: Lisa Dyer
Designer: Nigel Soper
Photographer: Lucy Pope
Stylists: Petra Boase and Jane McAllister
Production Controller: Janette Burgin

CARLTON
BOOKS

Contents

1

Ribbons, Trimmings & Feathers

Velvet, lace, feather, fur, fringe or sequin trimmings, all in different styles and textures, can be used to transform an item of clothing in a flash. Available from haberdashery departments and sewing stores, trims can conjure different effects. Lace adds instant romance; sequin or beaded trim with feathers is street-stylish and contemporary; and piping or rickrack gives a girly sweetness to outfits.

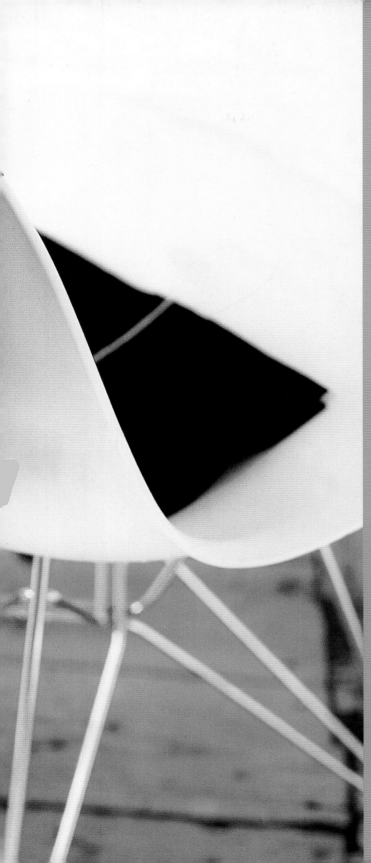

Pink-piped
Tuxedo
Trousers

Revisit the 1970s dance floor with these tuxedo-styled piped trousers. The tougher, more masculine image of tuxedos is married with shiny satin for a real disco-babe feel, making the trousers the perfect partywear for girls who hate skirts. This customizing idea would also work well for daywear by adding satin piping to the seams of jeans, chinos or pencil skirts.

WHAT YOU NEED
- Black satin trousers
- Tape measure
- Pale pink satin cord
- Scissors
- Pins
- Pale pink sewing thread
- Sewing needle

HOW TO DO IT
1 Place the trousers on a flat work surface and measure the side seam. Cut two lengths of pink cord to size, adding 15 mm (⅝ in) to each.

2 Starting at the top of one trouser side seam, turn under the end of the cord by 5 mm (¼ in) and pin it to abut the bottom of the waistband. Hand-sew it in place with a few couching stitches (see page 78).

3 Continue stitching the cord down the length of the seam with couching stitches. At the bottom of the trouser leg, turn the excess cord to the reverse of the hem and stitch in place.

4 Repeat steps 2 and 3 to stitch the piping on to the side seam of the other trouser leg.

Fake-fur
Cardigan

FAKE FUR ADDS a Zsa Zsa Gabor touch to clothing, transporting the most standard item into the high-glamour end of fashion. Whether you want to pretend you are an up-and-coming starlet or just like the way fur frames the face, fake-fur collars add luxe to a look. Attachable fur collars can be bought in different colours and sizes from sewing shops or notion stores; choose one that works with the collar on your cardigan.

WHAT YOU NEED
- Black cardigan with collar
- Brown fake-fur attachable collar
- Pins
- Brown sewing thread
- Scissors
- Sewing needle

HOW TO DO IT
Pin the fake-fur collar on to the right side of the cardigan collar. Hand-sew the collar in place, using a slip stitch (see page 79) and the brown thread.

Leopard-print Trousers

TAKE A WALK ON THE WILD SIDE with leopard-print trousers. Top-to-toe animal prints are usually best reserved for the ghetto-fabulous and famous – or an It girl on a paparazzi-popping night out, but you can still take part in the trend with the more subtle approach here. Trimming sugar-pink trousers with a leopard-print shows a lively attention-seeking attitude, but if you are fearful of heart, go more subtle by using black trousers.

WHAT YOU NEED
- Pink trousers
- Tape measure
- Scissors
- 5 cm (2 in) wide iron-on leopard-print hem tape
- Pins
- Iron and ironing board

HOW TO DO IT
1 Measure the trouser hem. Cut two lengths of leopard-print tape to size, adding 15 mm ($^5/_8$ in) to each.

2 Starting at the inside seam, pin each length of tape to a trouser leg, abutting the hem edge of the trousers. At the join, turn under the raw edge on one short end and neatly overlap on to the other end.

3 Place the trousers on an ironing or sleeve board and fuse one leg at a time. Following the manufacturer's instructions, cover the tape with a damp cloth and iron in place, removing the pins in each section as you work.

Flower &
Feather
Corsage

S HOULDERS ARE THE NEW erogenous zone to be tapped in the fashion stakes, and nothing makes a sexier silhouette than a one-shoulder top. The asymmetrical off-the-shoulder look is contemporary and provocative, especially when embellished with a shocking-pink corsage. Certain flowers have always denoted sexuality, and fake-flower corsages give an immediate allure, drawing attention to the face, breast, shoulder, waist or wherever you place them.

WHAT YOU NEED

- Pink feathers
- Pink fabric flower
- Pink sewing thread
- Sewing needle
- Scissors
- Large blank brooch pin
- Black stretchy one-shoulder top

HOW TO DO IT

1 Arrange the feathers in your hands and trim the quills to size. Here the feathers measure 15 cm (6 in) in length. Bind the ends of the quills by wrapping them with thread and knotting firmly.

2 Hand-sew the plumage on to the back of the fabric flower, using an overhand stitch (see page 79).

3 Hand-sew the brooch pin on to the back of the flower. To make the first knot, run the thread through one hole in the pin and into the flower, leaving an extra 'tail' of thread hanging. Knot the thread tightly to the hanging end, and then continue to stitch, wrapping the thread through the brooch pin and flower as you work. Knot to the previous stitches to secure. Repeat the procedure to secure the flower to the pin through the second hole.

4 Pin the corsage on to the shoulder of the top.

Glittery Pink-flower Top

WHAT YOU NEED
- Pink glittery v-neck top
- Pink fabric flower
- Pink sewing thread
- Sewing needle

HOW TO DO IT
Holding the flower firmly in place on the point of the 'v', slip-stitch it to the top (see page 79), working underneath the flower so that the stitches do not show.

Pink Rosebuds

Get into the baby-doll trend with puff sleeves and a candy pink sweetbriar neckline. Dress it down to keep the look fresh and modern. Frilly, feminine tops always look more chic-meets-street when paired with some dirty-and-lowdown denim jeans.

WHAT YOU NEED

- About 100 pink ribbon rosebuds
- Scissors
- Pink round-neck top
- Pink sewing thread
- Sewing needle

HOW TO DO IT

1 If your pink ribbon roses have green ribbon loops sewn on the reverse side (for leaves), remove them by snipping the attaching thread.

2 Starting on one shoulder seam, hand-sew a rosebud at the neckline, using a few slip stitches (see page 79) to secure it in place. Continue stitching on more roses, working around the inner edge of the neckline to the other shoulder seam, and stitching them as closely together as possible.

3 When you have completed the first row, repeat step 2 to stitch a second row of roses just outside the first.

Velvet & Rosebuds

UPDATE A PLAIN TOP with velvet and roses and make the everyday into the special occasion. This is for moments when you want to show your soft side. Paired with the right accessories and a skirt, the top can go from a wedding reception to a hot date, or anywhere in between. A plain strappy velvet top was used here to layer the two tones of green velvet, but you can choose a cotton or Lycra-mix version if you prefer.

WHAT YOU NEED

- Green velvet strappy top or camisole
- Tape measure
- Blue-green velvet trim
- Pins
- Blue-green and red sewing threads
- Sewing needle
- Scissors
- 7 red ribbon rosebuds

Tip
Use this trim idea along the hem of a skirt or a sweater to add romance. Roses can be stitched almost anywhere – into lace trims, on to sleeve cuffs or along the front opening of a pretty pastel cardigan.

HOW TO DO IT

1 Place the top on a flat work surface. Measure the length of the front neckline between the straps. Cut a length of velvet trim to size, adding 1 cm (½ in) for folding under the short ends.

2 Pin the trim flush to the neckline, folding under 5 mm (¼ in) at each short end. Hand-sew the ribbon in place along both long sides using a slip stitch (see page 79) and the blue-green thread. Remove the pins.

3 At approximately 2 cm (¾ in) intervals, hand-sew the ribbon rosebuds on to the velvet trim, using a tiny slip stitch and the red thread.

Feather
& Velvet Jeans

THE FEATHER TREND shows no signs of abating. Frills of feathers lend an ultra-fashionable look to clothes, which can be decadent and hip or invoke movie-star glamour from a bygone era. Taking inspiration from those Gucci jeans several years back, these feather-trimmed jeans belong to the first category by claiming a rock-chick cool. The feather-cuffed sweater, on the other hand, gives a feeling of retro luxe – anyone sporting these sleeves would certainly not be expected to wash dishes.

WHAT YOU NEED
- Jeans
- Tape measure
- Red feather trim
- 15 mm ($^5/_8$ in) wide red velvet ribbon
- Scissors
- Pins
- Sewing machine
- Red sewing thread

Feather-cuffed
Sweater

WHAT YOU NEED
- Black woollen or cotton sweater
- Ribbon-banded feather trim
- Pins
- Black sewing thread
- Sewing needle
- Scissors
- Tape measure

HOW TO DO IT

1 Measure around the sweater cuffs. Cut two lengths of ribbon-banded feather trim to size, adding 3 cm (1¼ in) on to each.

2 Turn the sweater wrong sides out. Starting at the seam of each cuff, pin the feather trim along the edge of the cuff, overlapping neatly at the seam to join.

3 Hand-sew the trim in place, through the edge of the feather band, using a slip stitch (see page 79). Add a few extra stitches at the join to secure firmly. Remove the pins and turn the sweater right sides out.

HOW TO DO IT

1 Place the jeans on a flat work surface and measure the hem. Cut two lengths each of feather trim and velvet ribbon to size, adding 1 cm (½ in) to each .

2 Pin a length of feather trim above the hem on the right side of each jeans leg so that the feathers rest along the bottom edge of the hem. Join the ends at the inside seam by neatly overlapping the trim.

3 Machine-stitch the trim in place on the right side of the jeans, using a straight stitch and red thread.

4 Add the velvet ribbon to both trouser legs. Pin the ribbon over the edge of the feather trim to conceal the stitching and ends. Join the ribbon ends at the inside seam by turning under one short end and overlapping it on to the other. Machine-stitch along both long sides of the ribbon, using a straight stitch.

Tied-ribbon Top

THE DELICATE FADED COLOURS and comfy thermal of this top provide a warm softness that is strokable and undeniably feminine. It is perfect for those times when you want to marry comfort with prettiness, whether you are cocooning at home or out-and-about on a warm spring day. A top with a lace-trimmed neckline is essential for adding the ribbon to the neckline.

WHAT YOU NEED

- Lilac thermal sleeveless top
- Blue sewing thread
- Sewing needle
- Scissors
- Small blue sequins
- Beading needle
- 7 mm (¼ in) wide pink velvet ribbon, about 80 cm (32 in) long
- Bodkin or large-eye needle

HOW TO DO IT

1 Place the thermal top on a flat work surface, front facing up. Using the pattern of the weave as a guide, hand-sew vertical lines of backstitch up the front of the top with blue thread. Here five equally spaced lines were made, each one varying in length.

2 Hand-sew one or two small blue sequins every 4 cm (1½ in) up each vertical line. To do this, first make a knot on the reverse side and bring the thread through to the front. Thread through the hole in the sequin, and then insert the needle through the top, as close to the sequin as possible, but on the outside edge. Repeat this, securing the next stitch at the other side of the sequin.

3 Thread the bodkin or large-eye needle with the velvet ribbon. Starting in the centre front of the top, evenly weave the ribbon in and out of gaps in the lace around the neckline. Tie the ends of ribbon in a bow.

Purple-trimmed Black Linen

CLEAN LINES ARE ENHANCED by a purple border, adding a certain preppy poise and pared-down elegance to a simple black linen dress. Classy and ladylike, the dress cries out for a summer garden party or a day at the races or the regatta. Any other colours of binding could be used; try edging the dress in white for that crisper, more cutting-edge, black-and-white effect seen on the catwalk.

WHAT YOU NEED

- Black linen dress
- Tape measure
- 2 cm (¾ in) wide purple satin bias binding
- Scissors
- Sewing machine
- Pins
- Sewing needle
- Tacking (basting) thread in a contrasting colour
- Purple sewing thread
- 30 cm (12 in) black cord
- Black sewing thread

HOW TO DO IT

1 Adapt the measurements for the bias binding you need according to the design of your dress. Cut out lengths of bias binding to size, adding 1 cm (½ in) to each. For the dress shown here, five lengths of binding were cut: one length for around the neckline; two lengths for the side sections of the dress; and two more for the back zip-to-side sections.

2 Starting at the back of the dress where the zip starts, insert the top of the dress into the seam of the folded binding, making sure that the raw edges of the binding are tucked under. Pin in place, and repeat to pin the bias binding lengths on to the other back zip-to-side seam edge, on to the sides and around the neckline. At each join, turn under one short end of the binding and overlap it on top of the other raw end.

3 Tack (baste) through both sides of the binding all around the dress to hold the binding in place.

4 Working on the right side of the dress, machine-stitch the binding in place, using a straight stitch and the purple thread. Remove the tacking (basting) stitches.

5 Cut the black cord in half and tie each half in a bow. Using the black thread, slip-stitch the bows (see page 79) on to the dress straps at the bias-binding ends.

Raspberry
Ribbon & Bead Cardigan

THE PLAINEST CARDIGAN can be jazzed up with frilly trim and beading to give a new romantic look. The top makes a warm wrap for floaty dresses or strappy camisoles, whether it is keeping shoulders warm in nippy weather or in ice-cold air conditioning. For a lively flash of colour glinting from the neckline, use a juicy lime or zesty lemon trim.

WHAT YOU NEED

· Raspberry-coloured cotton cardigan
· Tape measure
· 1 cm ($\frac{1}{2}$ in) wide ribbon frill trim, with the frill measuring 5 mm ($\frac{1}{4}$ in) deep
· Scissors
· Pins
· Tacking (basting) thread in a contrasting colour
· Sewing needle
· Red sewing thread
· 1 container (about 400) small red beads
· Beading needle

HOW TO DO IT

1 Measure the cardigan to work out how much ribbon you will need. Measure along the front opening from the bottom hem, around the neckline and down the length of the inner front opening. To this measurement, add 1 cm ($\frac{1}{2}$ in) for turning under the short ribbon ends.

2 Cut the ribbon to size and pin it to the reverse side of the cardigan along the front opening edges and the neckline. Turn under the short raw ends at the hem.

3 Tack (baste) the ribbon frill in place. Hand-sew the ribbon along the edges and neckline of the cardigan using a tiny hidden slip stitch (see page 79) and the red thread. Remove the tacking (basting) stitches.

4 Using the beading needle and red thread, sew red beads randomly along the front-opening panel and neckline. Sew each bead on separately, making two stitches through each one, and knotting securely.

Raffia-
trimmed Skirt

Shake your bon-bon à la Ricky Martin with a back-fringed skirt in hot pink. Get the Latino vibe pumping by mixing the skirt with a slinky top and flamenco dancing shoes, and hit the salsa clubs. Alternatively, go all country and cowgirl by working suede or leather fringing on to a denim skirt.

WHAT YOU NEED

· Pink cotton skirt
· Black raffia fringe trim
· Pins
· Black sewing thread
· 14-20 round metal studs
· Sewing machine
· Pins
· Scissors
· Tape measure

HOW TO DO IT

1 Place the skirt on a flat work surface, back facing up. Measure the back of the skirt where you want the raffia fringe. Here the fringing goes from side seam to side seam and is positioned at a slight 'v' curve, about 10 cm (4 in) from the waist at the deepest point.

2 Cut the raffia fringe trim to the back measurement, adding an extra 1 cm ($\frac{1}{2}$ in) for folding under the ends.

3 Fold under and pin both short ends of the trim by 5 mm ($\frac{1}{4}$ in). Pin the fringing in place on the skirt, curving slightly at the centre point to create the 'v'. Measure to ensure that the trim is equidistant from the waistband at both sides and the 'v' falls in the centre.

4 Machine-stitch the trim in place on the right side, about 5 mm ($\frac{1}{4}$ in) from the top edge of the raffia.

5 Insert the metal studs into the edge of the raffia, making sure they are equally spaced (see page 73). Following the manufacturer's instructions, firmly press a stud into the raffia from the right side. On the reverse side of the skirt, bend back the prongs with your fingers or a metal spoon to secure the stud.

Fluffy
Marabou Top

ANY VA-VA-VOOM PARTY GIRL will have an instant affinity with these come-hither bedroom looks that spell non-stop action. The trims are playful, conjuring up images of a silver-screen siren sipping a martini while lounging seductively in a swanky boudoir or jazz club. These two customizing designs will be sure to bring out the Mae West bad girl in you.

WHAT YOU NEED

- Black strappy top
- Tape measure
- Scissors
- Pale blue marabou trim
- Pins
- Pale blue sewing thread
- Sewing needle

HOW TO DO IT

1 Place the top on a flat work surface. Measure the straps and cut two lengths of marabou trim to size, adding 1 cm (½ in) to each. Measure along the top edge of the top and cut a length of marabou trim to size, adding 1 cm (½ in).

2 Pin the maribou trim to the straps and hand-sew in place along both long sides, using a slip stitch (see page 79) through the back of the trim. Remove the pins.

3 Starting at one side seam, pin marabou trim around the top edge, turning under neatly at the join and concealing the trim ends of the straps. Hand-sew the marabou trim in place along the top edge, using a small slip stitch, then remove the pins.

Fluoro Feathers

WHAT YOU NEED

- Sewing machine
- Pins
- 10 pink feathers
- Fluorescent pink sleeveless top
- Pink sewing thread
- Scissors

HOW TO DO IT

Pin the quill of each feather 5 mm (¼ in) below the edge of the neckline and 2 cm (¾ in) apart, working from shoulder seam to shoulder seam only. Machine-stitch the feathers 15 mm (⅝ in) in from the end of the quills, using a straight stitch. Trim the quill ends to neaten.

Rickrack Camisole

LINGERIE GETS OUT OF the bedroom with this charming rickrack trim. The black borders draw attention to the bustline, keeping the look sexy but sweet. Adding the black trim to different colours of camisole allows tops to be mixed with all those black basics in your wardrobe, thus extending the range of outfits on offer. The camisole looks especially good when worn under a tailored black trouser suit, giving a hint of seductiveness to power dressing.

WHAT YOU NEED

- Pink camisole
- Tape measure
- Wide and narrow black rickrack
- Scissors
- Sewing machine
- Pins
- Black sewing thread
- Sewing needle (optional)

Tip
For a different, more casual, effect, stitch rows of rickrack trim next to each other to create a multicoloured striped effect that will work well on T-shirts, along the hem of jeans or on denim handbags.

HOW TO DO IT

1 Place the camisole on a flat work surface. You will need four lengths of rickrack to cover this top, but adjust the amount you need according to the design.

2 Measure across the bottom bustline and cut a wide length of rickrack to size, adding 1 cm (½ in) for turning under the ends. Measure the top edge of the camisole, from the straps to the sides and across the back, and cut a length of narrow rickrack to size, plus 1 cm (½ in). Measure the v-neck, from the straps to the point of the 'v', and cut two lengths of rickrack to size, adding 1 cm (½ in); here the neckline is overlapped, so one piece of rickrack is longer than the other piece.

3 Starting at one side seam, pin the wide rickrack to the bustline seam, turning under the short ends by 5 mm (¼ in). Machine-stitch the rickrack in place along the centre of the trim, using a straight stitch. Alternatively, hand-sew in place with a running stitch.

4 Repeat step 3 to attach the narrow rickrack to the top edge and 'v' neckline of the camisole, aligning the rickrack with the edge of the camisole. Where each length joins, turn under one short end and overlap it on to the other end for a neat finish.

Pleated-ribbon Camisole

ADD THE HAUTE-COUTURE touch in the form of pleats to make a versatile camisole. Wear it demure and high class, in Audrey Hepburn mode, or downright trashy and over the top. Teamed with black satin trousers or a jet-beaded skirt, the top goes cocktail; pair it with a thigh-high-slashed skirt, and it says pure sex appeal.

WHAT YOU NEED

· Black camisole
· Tape measure
· Ready-pleated ribbon trim
· Black sequin trim
· Scissors
· Pins
· Black sewing thread
· Sewing needle

HOW TO DO IT

1 Place the camisole on a flat work surface and measure all the way around the top edge. Cut a length of both ribbon and sequin trims to size, adding 1 cm (½ in) to each for joining the ends.

2 Starting at one of the side seams, pin the pleated ribbon around the top edge of the camisole. Where the two ends meet, fold under one of the ends and overlap it on to the other end. Hand-sew the ribbon in place along the top edge, using a running stitch and the black thread. At the overlapped edge, sew a few slip stitches (see page 79) to secure the join. Remove the pins.

3 Starting at the same side seam, pin the sequin trim along the edge of the pleated ribbon, close to the edge of the neckline. To join the ends, overlap the short edges neatly. Hand-sew in place, using a running stitch, following the central machined stitching in the trim. Secure the overlapped ends with a few slip stitches. Remove the pins.

2

Beading
& Sequins

The jewel-like quality of beads and gemstones gives clothes a glamorous and exciting edge. A hem or seam can be decorated with diamantés or beads; a strap or cuff can be set sparkling with sequins; or an entire garment can be worked to create an ornate piece. Take care when washing garments that are embellished and avoid ironing over sequins, as they will melt.

Turquoise Indian
Mirror Top

ORNATE MIRROR SEQUINS give clothes an
exotic feel, and any colour combination
can be used. Multicoloured sequins work well
on a range of colours, but using the same
colour gives a more subtle effect. You need
only a few of these large embellished sequins
to create maximum impact.

WHAT YOU NEED

· Turquoise sleeveless top
· 14-16 Indian mirror sequins
  (28-32 if you are decorating
  the back as well)
· Chalk or pen fabric marker
· Turquoise sewing thread
· Scissors
· Sewing needle

HOW TO DO IT

1 Place the top on a flat surface, front facing up, and
arrange the sequins until you are happy with the overall
design. Here three sequins were placed above the
ribbed bottom, and the others were spaced randomly.

2 Using the chalk or fabric pen, mark a dot at the
points where you want to position each mirrored
sequin. Repeat on the back of the top, if desired.

3 Hand-sew the mirror sequins to the top at the
marked positions, using the turquoise thread. To do
this, knot the thread and, holding the sequin in place,
bring the thread through the embroidered edge of the
sequin from the reverse side of the top. Anchor with a
small straight stitch. Continue making stitches around
the edge of the sequin to secure it in place. If you like,
pin each sequin in place to fix it while you sew. Repeat
to attach all the sequins.

Sequinned Thermal Camisole

TAKE A BASIC CHAIN-STORE camisole top, available in a wide range of colours, and make it more upbeat by adding a dainty detailing of sequin trim and beads in a colour that complements the lace trim. No one will ever be able to tell that your inexpensive do-it-yourself version hasn't come from the trendiest boutique.

WHAT YOU NEED

- Grey lace-trimmed camisole with pink bow
- Tape measure
- Turquoise sequin trim
- Scissors
- Pins
- Turquoise and pink sewing threads
- Sewing needle
- About 50 turquoise glass bugle beads, measuring 5 mm (¼ in) long
- Beading needle

HOW TO DO IT

1 Measure along the neckline of the camisole, just under the lace trim. Cut a length of sequin trim to size, adding 1 cm (½ in).

2 Pin the sequin trim along the edge of the lace, turning under the raw ends at each side seam. If the trim is bulky, simply cut the ends flush with the side seam. Hand-sew the trim in place, using a slip stitch (see page 79).

3 Using the beading needle, hand-sew the turquoise beads onto the lace trim at different angles for a 'scattered' effect. Sew two stitches through each bead and knot on the reverse side of the camisole.

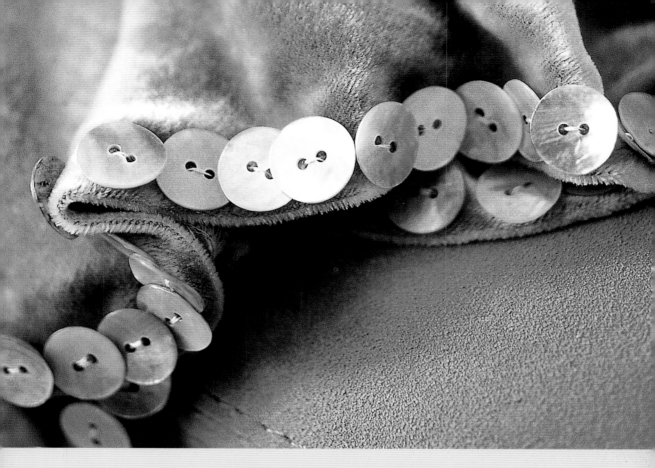

Velvet Button Skirt

SOMETIMES THE PRETTIEST embellishment is the easiest. Why pay a small fortune for a designer skirt trimmed with buttons, when it is so simple to create one yourself? Lustrous shell buttons beautifully highlight the sheen of the velvet and accentuate the soft, feminine look.

Tip

For a more elaborate effect, combine buttons of different colours and shapes – small buttons interspersed with larger ones, square shapes with hearts. Novelty buttons in animal shapes would look sweet on children's sweaters, jackets or dresses.

WHAT YOU NEED

- Pale mauve velvet skirt
- Shell or mother-of-pearl buttons, enough for the hem
- Tape measure
- Cream sewing thread
- Scissors
- Sewing needle

HOW TO DO IT

1 First make sure you have enough buttons to go all the way around the hem of the skirt. If you know how many buttons, side by side, fill a given measurement, such as five buttons for every 8 cm (3¼ in), you can work out how many you will need overall. Always have a few extra buttons spare.

2 Hand-sew a button on the hem of the skirt, making sure that the edge of the button abuts the hem and that the holes are parallel with it.

3 Continue to sew buttons along the edge, making sure they are as close as possible, with no space between them, and that they are all aligned. Here the buttons have been sewn on to overlap each other.

Beaded Argyll

THE UNEXPECTED COMBINATION of pretty pink beads with the Argyll pattern creates a modern classic. You can be a serious college girl without giving up one iota of girliness. Think New England in autumn with a shot of frivolity – and oh so much better than wearing pearls!

WHAT YOU NEED

- Blue Argyll wool sweater
- Ruler (optional)
- Chalk or pen fabric marker (optional)
- 1 container (about 400) pink glass beads
- Pink sewing thread
- Scissors
- Sewing needle
- Tacking (basting) thread
- Beading needle

HOW TO DO IT

1 Place the sweater on a flat work surface, front facing up. Decide where you want the lines of beads. The easiest method is to follow the existing pattern, working along the thin crisscrossing lines.

2 Alternatively, use the ruler and fabric marker to measure and mark out lines following the diagonal but halfway through the squares or parallel to the crisscrossing lines. Then sew a line of tacking (basting) stitches, regularly using a ruler to make sure that the lines are exactly straight. Before you start sewing, check the effect from a distance.

3 Hand-sew the beads in place, following one diagonal line, or one tacked (basted) line, at a time. Sew each bead on separately, making two stitches through each one, and knot the thread securely on the reverse side. As you work, carefully abut each bead to the one before to make a continuous line, unbroken by spaces.

Beaded Heart Sweater

THE PERFECT SYMMETRY of the heart makes it an ideal motif for all kinds of decorative arts. This ancient symbol for love is worked on to the front and sleeves of a sweater for a romantic effect. Asymmetrical or elongated hearts are also good for creating a look that is more stylized.

WHAT YOU NEED

- Grey wool or cotton sweater
- Pen or chalk fabric marker
- Tape measure
- About 120 pale pink glass beads
- Grey sewing thread
- Beading needle

Tip

Hearts are not the only shape that are simple in design yet potent in meaning. You could substitute stars, diamonds, a basic flower shape or even a sun or large asterisk combined with shorter, disconnected, beaded 'rays'.

HOW TO DO IT

1 Measure and mark the outline of a heart centrally below the neckline on the front of the sweater using the chalk or pen marker. To make sure the heart is centred, fold the sweater in half with the back sides together; the centre of the heart should fall on the centre foldline . It can be any size you like; here the heart measures 2.5 cm (1 in).

2 Thread the beading needle with the grey thread, knot it, then bring it through from the reverse side of the sweater at the bottom tip of the heart. Thread on the first bead, re-enter the sweater along the marked line and repeat to make two stitches, then knot on the reverse. Continue sewing on the beads close together, following the marked line.

3 Repeat steps 1 and 2 to make hearts on the sleeves or, if desired, another on the back of the sweater.

Glitzy Denim Jacket

THINK RHINESTONE COWBOY and decorate a plain denim jacket with sequin trims and a confetti of coloured gemstones. This version uses predominately turquoise and pink, but you could try red and black for a hard-edged look, or whatever combination works with the colours in your wardrobe.

WHAT YOU NEED

· Denim jacket
· 1 pink sequin appliqué leaf
· Pins
· Pink and turquoise sewing threads
· Sewing needle
· Tape measure
· Scissors
· Double-width turquoise sequin trim
· Pink sequin trim
· Turquoise metallic cord
· Chalk or pen fabric marker
· 5 red and 5 pink gemstone star beads
· Clear 'invisible' thread
· Beading needle
· 60 round gemstone studs in assorted colours

HOW TO DO IT

1 Place the denim jacket, front facing up, on a flat work surface. Position the sequin appliqué leaf on one collar lapel and pin it in place. Then use a slip stitch (see page 79) and the pink thread to hand-sew around the edge of the appliqué leaf to secure it.

2 Measure all the way around the edge of the collar and cut a length of double turquoise sequin trim to size. Starting at one corner, pin the trim in place around the back of the collar, flush with the edge. When you reach the other corner, cut off the surplus trim flush with the edge. Then pin the trim along the two short lengths of the collar, butting the ends together. Hand-sew the sequin trim in place along both long sides, using a slip stitch and the turquoise thread.

3 Measure the horizontal seams above the pockets on both sides of the jacket and cut two lengths of pink sequin trim to size, adding 1 cm (½ in) to each. Working from the side seams in, pin the lengths in place, overlapping the trim on to the reverse of the central fastening. Hand-sew in place, using the pink thread and following the central machined stitching in the trim.

4 Measure the edge of the pocket flap and cut two lengths of turquoise metallic cord to size. Slip stitch a length of cord to the edge of each pocket flap, using the turquoise thread. Secure each end with a few overhand or couch stitches (see pages 78-9) to prevent fraying.

5 Hand-sew the red and pink star beads to the lapels of the collar. Use the fabric marker to make dots on the collar where you want the stars to be positioned. Sew on each bead separately, making two stitches through each one and knotting securely on the reverse side.

6 Add a sprinkling of coloured gemstone studs over the top panel of the jacket on both sides. If desired, mark positions for the gemstones, as for the stars in step 5; otherwise, place them randomly. To insert each gemstone, push the pronged piece through the denim from the reverse side (see page 73). Insert the gemstone into the centre and bend the prongs around the stone.

Glitzy
Red sequins

GO FROM DAY TO NIGHT by giving a sexy touch to a classic, demure poloneck (turtleneck) with sequin edging, showing there's more to be discovered behind your well-behaved ladylike exterior. An ideal top for when you need to present a refined elegance but don't want to look boring.

WHAT YOU NEED
- Red poloneck (turtleneck)
- Tape measure
- Narrow red sequin trim
- Scissors
- Pins
- Red elastic thread
- Sewing needle

TAKE A POLONECK (TURTLENECK) SWEATER THAT YOU HAVE TIRED OF

HOW TO DO IT

1 Measure the cuffs and neck edge of the sweater and cut three lengths of sequin trim to size, adding 1 cm (½ in) to each.

2 Pin the sequin trim to the right side of the sweater at the edges of the cuffs and the folded-over edge of the neck. Join the trim ends at the seams by overlapping.

3 Hand-sew the sequin trim in place, using the elastic thread. Make tiny running stitches, following the central machined stitching in the trim.

Strappy Sequin LBD

STRAPPY, BARELY-THERE little black dresses never go out of fashion, but even they can look a little uninspiring and in need of a lift after you have worn them a zillion times. Hand-sew sequin-covered trim in place so that you can unpick it later if you wish and revert to your unadorned original.

WHAT YOU NEED
- Black strappy satin dress
- Scissors
- Tape measure
- 1 cm (½ in) wide red velvet ribbon
- Black sewing thread
- Pins
- Sewing needle
- Black sequin trim

HOW TO DO IT

1 Remove the straps of the dress by unpicking the stitching or carefully cutting them away. Measure the straps and replace them with two lengths of red velvet ribbon cut to the same size. Pin and machine- or hand-stitch the ribbons in place on the reverse side.

2 Measure all the way around the top edge of the dress. Cut a length of sequin trim to size, adding 1 cm (½ in) for joining the ends. Pin the sequin trim around the top of the dress, joining the ends at a side seam by turning them under and abutting the short raw ends.

3 Hand-sew the sequin trim to the dress using a tiny slip stitch (see page 79) along both long edges of the trim.

GLAMORIZE THAT LITTLE BLACK DRESS THAT HAS PROVED SO USEFUL BUT NEEDS A LIFT

Tip
These dangling jewelled sequins will add instant eye-catching glamour when they are stitched along the cuffs and hem of a little black cardigan or crocheted top. Alternatively, sew them along the hem of a skirt or cropped black trousers for another fun and jazzy eveningwear idea.

Beaded Satin Trousers

A SPRINKLING OF CANDY-COLOURED beads looks good enough to eat. They add just enough decoration to give a pair of blue-grey tailored trousers some spanking new groove. The bright red, yellow, white and blue beads not only liven up the grey colour, but also provide textural relief to the satin fabric.

WHAT YOU NEED
- Blue-grey satin trousers
- 400 round and straight small glass beads, in assorted colours
- Blue-grey sewing thread
- Beading needle
- Scissors
- Tape measure

HOW TO DO IT

1 Starting at the hem of one trouser leg, sew on assorted coloured and shaped beads in a triangular formation, using the beading needle and the blue-grey thread. Here the triangle measured 8 x 10 cm (3 x 4 in), with the centre of the triangle on the seam. Sew each bead on with two stitches, knotting securely on the reverse side of the trousers.

2 Once you have sewn the beaded triangle shape, sew a line of beads up the side seam of the trouser leg. Here about 200 beads were used per leg.

3 Repeat steps 1 and 2 on the other trouser leg.

Diamanté Jeans

TRIM WITH TINY DIAMANTÉ studs decorates the side seams of bootleg jeans, giving rock-chick styling to a wardrobe basic. The eye-catching sparkly gems instantly elevate these jeans to hot partywear – just team them with a skimpy top and strappy heels for effortless glamour. Even better, the vertical line helps make the leg look longer.

WHAT YOU NEED

- Jeans
- Tape measure
- Diamanté trim
- Scissors
- Pins
- Black sewing thread
- Sewing needle

Tip

Use the same approach for the side seams of black trousers or a pencil skirt. This type of delicate diamanté trim could also be sewn in parallel horizontal lines around a skirt or worked in diagonals across it.

HOW TO DO IT

1 Measure the side seam of the jeans and cut two lengths of diamanté trim to size, adding 1 cm (½ in) to each.

2 Starting just below the waistband, pin the trim down the side seams of the jeans, from flush with the bottom of the waistband, and turning the overlap under at the bottom hem.

3 Hand-sew the trim in place along both long edges, using a slip stitch (see page 79) and the black thread.

Leopard-
print-lined Skirt

EVERY GIRL NEEDS a hot little number for dates, parties and playtime. Vamp it up with sequins and super-sexy leopardskin that will look seductive whether you are perching on a barstool or sashaying through a dark nightclub. Wear this skirt with a matching camisole and vertiginous heels to bring out the animal in you.

WHAT YOU NEED

- Side-slit straight black wool skirt
- Scissors
- Tape measure
- Leopard satin lining fabric, pre-washed and pressed
- Sewing machine
- Pins
- Iron and ironing board
- Black thread
- Black sequin trim
- Sewing needle

HOW TO DO IT

1 Remove the original lining from the skirt by unpicking the seams. To calculate how much leopardskin fabric you will need for the lining, first measure the length and then the width of each piece of original lining, including all the seam allowances and hems. Add up the total length and total width to get the final measurement. If in doubt, always purchase more fabric than you think you will need.

2 Use the pieces of original lining as a pattern to cut out the leopardskin fabric. Press the pieces flat, then pin them right-sides down on to the reverse side of the leopardskin fabric, aligning them with the fabric grain. Cut out the pieces, allowing for any seam allowance or hem that you were unable to unpick.

Tip

Try lining a simple, chic black skirt with vibrant purple, hot pink or red satin for a more sophisticated, less vampish look. If you prefer, the lining can be hand-sewn along the side slits rather than left hanging, as shown here.

3 Turn under and press the seam allowance on all pieces. Machine-stitch the pieces together along the long side seams. Follow the original lining as a guide; for example, if the skirt has a zip, stitch only as far along the seam as the zip; if it has a side slit, stitch only to that point. Press the seams open on the stitched areas.

4 Before you attach the new lining, stitch the sequin trim to the skirt. Turn the skirt right-sides out. Measure the side seams from the waist to the slits and cut two lengths of black sequin trim to size, adding 1 cm ($\frac{1}{2}$ in) to each. Pin a length of sequin trim down each side seam, and turn under the raw ends. Hand-sew the trim in place, using a running stitch and following central machined stitching in the trim.

5 Turn the skirt reverse sides out and pin the lining to the skirt at the waistband seam, aligning it with the zip and side seams. At the zip, fold under the seam allowance on the lining and pin neatly to the zip tape. Hang the skirt up and check that the lining hangs straight, is smooth and doesn't pucker.

6 Slip-stitch the lining to the skirt along the waistband and then to the zip tape, taking care not to sew through to the right side of the skirt.

7 At each slit, fold under the seam allowance twice and pin it in place (you will need to cut into the seam allowance at the top of the slit). At the bottom hem, turn under the seam allowance twice, mitre the corners at the slit sides and pin in place. Check and adjust the length of the hem if necessary. Hand-hem all the raw edges along the bottom edge and slits of the skirt to finish. The lining hangs free at the slits and hem.

Pink Sequin
Camisole

DANCE THE NIGHT AWAY wearing this sequinned top and you'll outsparkle the disco mirrorball. Nothing is sexier and slinkier than lingerie-style camisoles in vibrant eatable colours, like this luscious juicy pink. The shimmering sequinned detailing screams 'look at me'.

WHAT YOU NEED
- Pink cotton camisole
- Tape measure
- Scissors
- Pink sequin trim
- Pins
- Pink sewing thread
- Sewing needle

HOW TO DO IT

1 Measure the straps of the camisole and cut two lengths of pink sequin trim to size, adding 1 cm (½ in) to each.

2 Measure around the top edge of the camisole and cut another length of the sequin trim to size, adding 1 cm (½ in) to the measurement.

3 Pin the sequin trim to the straps, turning under each short end by 5 mm (¼ in). Hand-sew the trim in place, using pink thread and a running stitch and following the central machined stitching line in the trim.

4 In the same way, pin and hand-sew the sequin trim around the neckline of the camisole. Join the ends at one side seam, turning under one short end and overlapping it on to the other.

Tip

If you have a black cardigan that's crying out for decoration, think modern and go for red beads with animal-print lining or white beads with ivory.

Turquoise
Beaded
Cardigan

BE A 1950S SWEATER GIRL in this pastel beaded cardigan, which is the perfect foil to the sharp lines of a pencil skirt or can be teamed with flirty skirts and romantic chiffon dresses. Simply drape it over your shoulders and fasten a single button.

WHAT YOU NEED

- 80–100 straight turquoise glass beads, 3 cm (1¼ in) long
- Turquoise thread
- Beading needle
- Scissors
- Pink round-necked cardigan
- Pattern paper and pencil, or 1 m (39 in) of 115 cm- (45 in-) wide calico (muslin)
- Chalk or pen fabric marker
- 1 m (39 in) of 115 cm- (45 in-) wide turquoise satin lining, pre-washed and pressed
- Tape measure
- Pins
- Iron and ironing board
- Pink thread
- Sewing needle

HOW TO DO IT

1 Sew clusters of beads to the front of the cardigan. To do this, thread the beading needle with turquoise thread and knot the end. Make several small stitches through the front of the cardigan and knot them together on the reverse side. Then stitch through the cardigan and thread on 3–4 turquoise beads. Re-enter the same hole, come up again, and thread through one of the beads then back through the same hole, securing the cluster by knotting through the threads on the reverse side. Repeat the process to make 10–15 clusters on each side of the front of the cardigan.

2 Turn the cardigan wrong reverse out and place it on a flat work surface. Now you need to make three pattern template pieces for the lining: two for the sides and one for the back. The sleeves will not be lined.

3 Starting with one of the sides, pin the pattern paper or calico (muslin) to the reverse side and use a pen or pen fabric marker to mark along the seams and about 2 cm (¾ in) from the bottom edge. Cut out the pattern and check that it follows the shape of the side piece of the cardigan and is flush with the front opening and neckline. The piece should be the exact size of the

finished lining for that section of the cardigan. Mark the top side. Repeat to make pattern pieces for the opposite side and the back.

4 Pin the three pattern pieces, top sides down, to the reverse side of the turquoise lining fabric, aligning them with the fabric grain. Using chalk or a pen fabric marker, mark around the template, adding 1 cm (½ in) seam allowance all around. Cut out each piece.

5 Turn under and press the seam allowance on all sides of each piece of the lining. Clip the armhole sections halfway through the seam allowance only, to help them fit smoothly around the curves.

6 Working on a side piece first, pin the lining, right side facing up, to the inside of the cardigan, making sure the fabric fits smoothly. Using the pink thread, neatly slip-stitch the lining in place (see page 79) along all the edges and making sure the stitches only catch the wool so that they do not appear on the right side.

7 Repeat step 6 to attach the other side piece and then the back piece, abutting the pieces flush with each other where they join .

Rays of Light

A PALE BLUE CORDUROY SKIRT is 'dressed up' with rows of light-catching silver sequins, worked from the hem upward in strips of various lengths. Wear it cowboy-style with snakeskin boots and a denim jacket, or go for a more feminine approach with blue fishnets and a sequinned top. Narrow-ribbed corduroy is more flattering than wide-whale.

WHAT YOU NEED

- 1.5 m (60 in) silver sequin trim
- Scissors
- Blue corduroy skirt
- Pins
- Silver thread
- Chalk or pen fabric marker and ruler (optional)
- Sewing machine
- Sewing needle (optional)

HOW TO DO IT

1 Cut the sequin trim into several different lengths, ranging from 12 cm (4 ¾ in) to 24 cm (9 ½ in). Place the skirt on a flat work surface and arrange the lengths in vertical rows from the hem. You can either make a pattern by alternating short, medium and long lengths in different spacings, or just arrange them randomly until you like the design.

2 Pin the lengths of sequin trim in place on the skirt with the ends flush with the hem. The pattern of the corduroy will help you position the lengths straight. Alternatively, use a ruler and fabric marker to make vertical lines and then cut the sequin trim to match.

3 Machine-stitch each length of sequin trim in place with a running stitch, following the central machined stitching in the trim. Sew toward the hem so that you can hold the trim taut to keep it straight. Alternatively, use a zigzag stitch set to the width of the trim, or hand-sew the trim in place, using a running stitch.

Indian
Goddess
T-shirt

AN INDIAN GODDESS image is decorated with a profusion of sequins and beads, creating a multicoloured one-of-a-kind effect. If you can't find a similar T-shirt, take an image you like to a colour-copy or T-shirt transfer printing shop and ask for it to be transfer-printed on to a white T-shirt. You could choose a picture of your own 'goddess' – Madonna or Britney, perhaps (a favourite rock-concert T-shirt can get a new lease of life this way).

WHAT YOU NEED

- White cotton T-shirt with 'goddess'-type design
- Cardboard
- 150 assorted sequins and 100 assorted beads
- Clear 'invisible' thread, or coloured sewing threads
- Beading needle
- Scissors
- Ruler
- Chalk or pen fabric marker

HOW TO DO IT

1 Place the T-shirt on a flat work surface and slip a piece of cardboard inside it to prevent you stitching through to the other side.

2 Arrange beads and sequins on the design to highlight different areas. Hand-sew each one in place with a few stitches, knotting securely on the reverse of the T-shirt. For a more layered effect, sew smaller sequins on top of large ones or use sparkly beads to anchor the sequins (the bead will need to be bigger than the sequin hole). Bring the thread through the sequin, then thread on a bead and re-enter through the same hole in the sequin, knotting on the reverse side.

3 Using the fabric marker and a ruler, draw a faint square frame 5 cm (2 in) from the edge of the printed image. Sew an assortment of different sequins in various colours, shapes and sizes along the sides of the frame. Stitch an intersecting series of long straight beads, small round sequins and larger sequins to link the square outline frame with the printed image.

Flirty Frilled Skirt

THE CLASSIC SEAMSTRESS'S method of lengthening skirts is given a new slant with a chiffon ra-ra edge and sequin trim. This fun, flippy skirt, adapted from a red bias-cut version, presents a flirty romantic look, marrying heavier, sophisticated, velvet with springy, youthful, chiffon. The sequin trim can be in a colour to match the skirt, or in silver, gold or a contrasting colour.

WHAT YOU NEED

- Red velvet skirt
- Tape measure
- Red chiffon
- Scissors
- Pins
- Sewing machine
- Red sewing thread
- Pink sequin trim
- Sewing needle

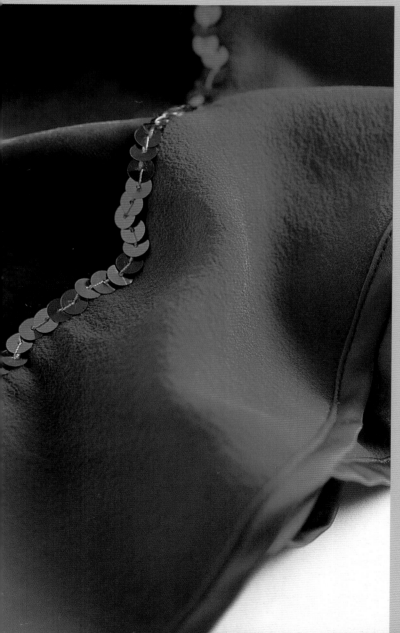

HOW TO DO IT

1 Place the skirt on a flat work surface and unpick the hem to reveal the raw edges. Measure around the circumference of the hem. Cut a length of chiffon on the bias to this measurement, adding an 3 cm (1¼ in). The chiffon frill can be any width you like, depending on the length you want the skirt to be; here the frill measures 15 cm (6 in) deep.

2 Fold the chiffon strip in half lengthways, right sides facing, and pin the short raw edges together. Slide the band on to the hem of the skirt to check that it fits, leaving a seam allowance of 1.5 cm (⅝ in) for the short ends to be joined.

3 Remove the chiffon band, adjust as necessary, and machine-stitch the short ends together, right sides facing, to make a band. Overlock the raw edges of the seam allowance with a zigzag stitch.

4 Pin the chiffon band on to the bottom of the skirt with right sides together and long raw edges aligned. Make sure the joined ends of the chiffon band are at one of the skirt's side seams. Machine-stitch the chiffon to the skirt. Overlock the raw edges of the seam allowance with a zigzag stitch to prevent fraying.

5 Open out the chiffon band and press along the seam on the right side. Cut a length of sequin trim measuring the circumference of the skirt along the join of the chiffon. Pin in place to cover the stitched seam, joining the ends by turning under one short end and overlapping it on to the other at a side seam. Hand-sew the trim in place along both long edges, using a running stitch and the red thread, and following the central machined stitching in the trim.

6 Turn under, press and pin a narrow double hem along the raw edge of the chiffon. Machine-stitch the hem in place or hand-sew, using a slip stitch (see page 79).

Sweetheart T-shirt

A RIBBON-AND-BEAD TRIM in candy pink transforms a plain white T-shirt into the sweetest top, perfect for wearing with capris or lightweight skirts in summer. Do, however, choose a close-fitting T-shirt for the best results, perhaps with short sleeves, as here, or with three-quarter sleeves. A loose shirt, or one with ribbing or a wide band around the neck or sleeves, is too sporty-looking for such a delicate treatment as this.

WHAT YOU NEED

- White cotton v-neck T-shirt
- 1.5 cm (⅝ in) wide pink satin ribbon
- Tape measure
- Pins
- About 200 small pink glass bugle beads
- 1 heart gemstone
- Pink sewing thread
- Scissors
- Sewing needle
- Beading needle

HOW TO DO IT

1 Measure the distance around the neckline, and cut a length of pink satin ribbon to size, adding about 10 cm (4 in) for turning under the ends and fitting.

2 Turn under one short end of the ribbon and pin it to point of the 'v'. Pin the ribbon along the edge of the neckline, easing it around all corners. At the end, trim the ribbon if necessary and turn under the short end, pinning it in place to abut the other end. There will be a slight gathering along the inner side of the ribbon as it is eased, but this is part of the effect.

3 Hand-sew the ribbon trim in place along both long sides, using a slip stitch (see page 79). Remove the pins.

4 Hand-sew the pink bugle beads on to the ribbon at different angles for a 'scattered' effect. Nestle some into the folds of the ribbon. Sew two stitches through each bead and knot on the reverse of the T-shirt.

5 Finish by sewing a heart gemstone on the point of the 'v' to conceal the join.

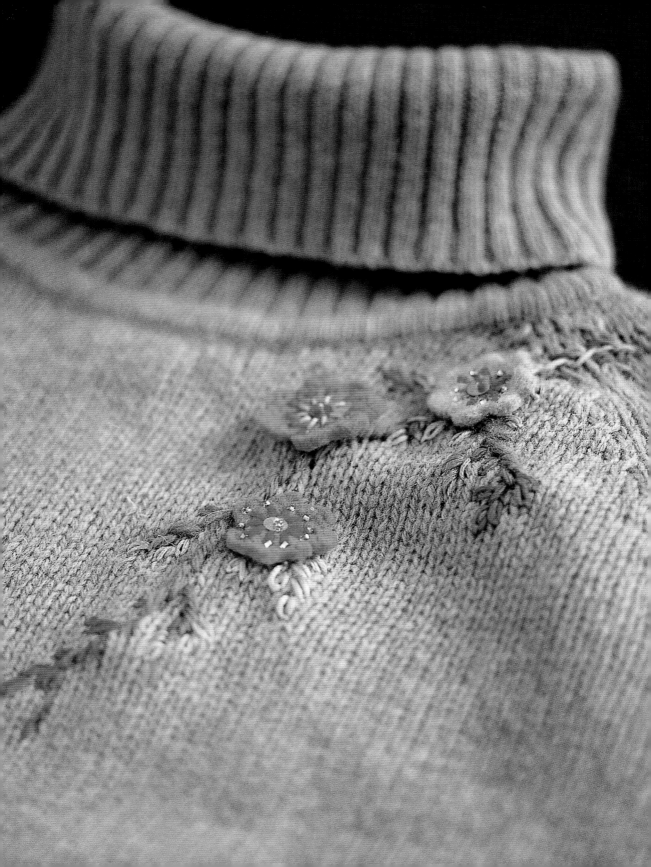

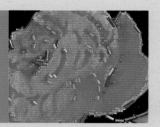

3

Appliqué & Embroidery

Appliqué is simply the process of stitching or bonding one shape of fabric on to another. Fusible webbings make the technique fast, easy and super-effective. Appliqué motifs, whether representational or abstract, can be used as decoration on their own or as a starting point for further embellishment. Embroidery adds a rich texture to clothing that can look as sublime or overstated as you like.

Bunch of
Red Roses

FOR THIS DESIGN you will need a flower patterned fabric with huge full-blown blooms on it. Here a rose-print headscarf was used, but if you can't find roses, look for poppies or any other large red flower. Search secondhand and thrift shops for suitable fabric, or look at roll-ends of upholstery fabric on sale. Pansies or violets will look striking on a purple top, but as they are usually printed smaller, you may need more of them. A 'virtual garden' of peonies will make an intensely lush design.

WHAT YOU NEED

· Flowered fabric with at least 5 large roses
· Paper-backed fusible webbing
· Iron and ironing board
· Embroidery scissors
· Red cotton top with three-quarter sleeves
· Pins
· 5 green or black gemstone studs

HOW TO DO IT

1 Following the webbing manufacturer's instructions, iron a length of webbing to the reverse side of the patterned fabric (see page 76).

2 Cut out the rose shapes with the embroidery scissors, cutting around and into all the detail of leaves and petals. Here five shapes were cut out. Peel the paper backing off each rose.

3 Place the top on the ironing board and arrange the roses on the front. When you are happy with the positioning of the pieces, pin them in place. Iron each one by covering with a cloth and pressing the iron on top, according to the webbing manufacturer's instructions. Allow the top to cool.

4 Insert a gemstone stud into the centre of each rose (see page 73). Push the pronged piece through the fabric from the reverse side. Insert the gemstone into the centre and bend the prongs around the stone with your fingers or a metal spoon to secure it.

Abstract Flower

BREAK UP A GEOMETRIC monochrome with a bright abstracted floral. A chequerboard pattern makes the perfect contrasting background for something curvy, feminine, vibrant and glittery. Black-and-white stripes, op-art gyroscopes, zigzags or chevrons would all be good alternatives. This is a top that delivers a powerful visual punch, so you need attitude to wear it – it's definitely not one for the wallflowers.

TAKE ONE BLACK-AND-WHITE SWEATER ...

WHAT YOU NEED

- Fabric with a print of a large flower
- Paper-backed fusible webbing
- Iron and ironing board
- Embroidery scissors
- Black-and-white checked sweater
- Large green glass bead
- Green sewing thread
- Small flat-backed gemstones or diamantés
- Fabric glue

HOW TO DO IT

1 Following the webbing manufacturer's instructions, iron the paper-backed webbing on to the reverse side of the flower-patterned fabric (see page 76).

2 Cut out the flower shape with the embroidery scissors, cutting around and into all the detail of the leaves and flower petals.

3 Place the sweater on the ironing board and check the position for the flower. Here the rose has been positioned in the upper right-hand corner. Peel the paper backing off the flower, place in position, cover with a cloth and iron according to the webbing manufacturer's instructions. Allow to cool.

4 Hand-sew a glass bead in the centre of the flower with green thread. Place a dab of fabric glue on the back of one of the gemstones and stick to one of the petals. Repeat to stick gemstones on other petals.

Zebraskin 'N' Flowers

ADD FLAIR TO A CASUAL TOP with zebra stripes, dotted with appliqué flowers. The curvy shapes of floral blooms help break up the harder lines of black and white. Using an initial stops the design from being too girly. Suede tape is available in a range of finishes and patterns, so use your imagination to combine it with your existing clothes and accessories. Try using it to create jazzy borders on bags, or to trim cuffs. The flowers can be purchased as ready-made appliqués, or cut out from a decorative ribbon or fabric remnant.

WHAT YOU NEED

- Iron-on zebraskin suede tape, measuring 3 cm (1¼ in) wide
- Lime-green sleeveless cotton top
- Scissors
- Pins
- Tape measure or ruler
- Iron and ironing board
- 4 ready-made embroidered appliqué roses
- Fabric glue

HOW TO DO IT

1 Cut out strips of the iron-on fabric tape to make the letter of your choice. Any letter with straight lines is suitable: A, E, F, H, K, L, M, N, T, V, W, X, Y or Z. Here 35 cm (13¾ in) of tape was used to make a 12 cm (4¾ in) high letter N.

2 Place the top flat on the ironing board and arrange the zebraskin tape pieces to form the letter. Pin the pieces in place, measuring to check that the letter is straight and centred.

3 Following the manufacturer's instructions, cover the tape with a cloth and iron in place, removing the pins in each section as you work. Allow to cool.

4 Position the four embroidered roses on the letter. Here they have been placed at each corner of the letter. When you are happy with their position, glue each one in place with fabric glue. Allow to dry.

Glitter Heart & Wings

COOL CLUBWEAR TO DANCE the night away – team this angel-heart top with some skinny hip-huggers and a pair of sexy strappy shoes for that oh so rock-chick look. Combine velvet appliqué pieces with leopardskin or suede, then accent with glitter or sequins.

HOW TO DO IT

1 To make templates for the design, draw a heart on to the cardboard, then draw two wings – a right one and a left one – and cut out the three templates.

2 Place a piece of the fusible webbing on a work surface and lay the scrap of pink satin for the heart on top, right side up (see page 75). Pin together. Place the template on top, trace around it with the fabric marker, then cut out the heart shape through both layers. Repeat the process to cut out the two wings from the leopardskin fabric and webbing. Treat each shape as one piece.

3 Alternatively, if you use paper-backed fusible webbing, you can iron-fuse the webbing to the wrong side of the fabric, draw the shapes directly on to the paper side, cut out and then peel off the paper before fusing it in place (see Bunch of Red Roses, pages 54-5).

4 Place the top on the ironing board and centre the heart on the front, making sure that the fusible webbing is exactly aligned underneath and the design is centred. Following the webbing manufacturer's instructions, carefully place a cloth over the heart and hold a hot iron on top until the cloth is dry. Do not slide the iron back and forth. Lift the cloth off. Repeat to iron on the wings, abutting them neatly to the sides of the heart.

5 Machine-stitch around the heart and wing shapes, using a close zigzig stitch. Use pink thread for the heart and black thread for the wings.

6 Place the top on a flat work surface. Cover the heart with a generous amount of fabric glue, using the paintbrush to spread it evenly (see page 74). Sprinkle on the sequins. Leave to dry overnight. To finish, shake the top on to newspaper to remove any loose sequins.

WHAT YOU NEED

- Cardboard and pen
- Scissors
- Chalk or pen fabric marker
- Fusible webbing
- Pins
- Scrap of bright pink satin for the heart
- Scraps of leopard-print satin
- Red cotton strappy top
- Pink and black sewing threads
- Fabric glue for sequins and glitter
- Paintbrush
- Machine-washable pink heart sequins
- Iron and ironing board
- Sewing machine
- Scissors

THE POPULAR FASHION for adding decoration to the hems of jeans takes a twist here with leather and tweed. Cut-outs in buttery cream and chocolate-brown leather complement the tailored look of brown tartan trousers, giving pretty detailing to a classic style. If you can't afford Bottega Veneta, or cleverly cut Joseph leather trousers, inexpensive leather scraps can be cut out in any shape and size you like and patched-and-pieced to thick felt handbags, tweedy skirts or even Burberry-style checked scarves.

Leather-detailed Checked Trousers

WHAT YOU NEED

- Cardboard and pen
- Scissors
- Scraps of leather in cream and chocolate
- Brown tartan-checked tweed trousers
- Pins
- Ochre and brown stranded cotton embroidery threads
- Embroidery needle
- Tape measure
- Beading needle
- Clear 'invisible' thread
- 12-14 yellow or clear beads
- 30-40 small flat-backed gemstones
- Strong fabric glue

HOW TO DO IT

1 Make two cardboard templates for the flowers by drawing a large and a small flower shape freehand on to the cardboard and cutting them out. Here the cream flowers measure 8 x 10 cm (3 x 4 in) and the brown flowers are 5 x 8 cm (2 x 3 in).

2 Trace around the large template on to the back of the cream leather, then trace around the small one on to the back of the brown leather. Cut out and repeat to make two flowers in each colour and size.

3 Place the trousers on a flat work surface and position one cream and one brown flower cut-out on to the end of each trouser leg, measuring to match the positioning on both legs. When you are happy with the positions of the cut-outs, pin them in place.

4 Insert a piece of card inside one leg to prevent stitching through to the other side. Using one strand of embroidery thread, tack (baste) the leather flowers in place with short seed stitches (see page 78). Repeat on the other trouser leg to secure the leather cut-outs.

5 Using the beading needle, attach several beads to the centre of each flower. Secure each bead with two stitches through the leather and fabric.

6 Insert a piece of cardboard inside the trouser legs to make stitching easier. Using one strand of embroidery thread in ochre and brown, embroider around each flower with assorted stitches. Here a stem stitch was combined with large daisychain stitches (see page 78) to make the stems and leaf shapes. You may also like to try other embroidery stitches, such as feather or fern stitches (see page 78).

7 To finish, glue a scattering of small coloured and clear gemstones around the flowers and on to the trouser fabric with strong fabric glue (see page 73). Apply a dab of fabric glue to the reverse side of each gemstone and stick in place. Work one trouser leg at a time, allowing the first to dry before repeating on the other leg.

Pink Poodle

UPDATE THE 1950S CLASSIC American poodle skirt with an appliquéd and embroidered poodle pet on a bubble-gum pink sweater. It is a little nod to the days of bobby socks, ponytails, fluffy sweaters, full skirts and saddle shoes. Or think of it as an LA moment and make your appliqué a carbon copy of your own real dog; talking your dog for a walk while wearing the sweater could be just so California kitsch. Another variation is to make a giant dog face from brown felt, transfer it to the centre front of a sweatshirt and decorate with studs for the collar, embroidered details and glittery diamanté eyes.

WHAT YOU NEED

- Pink brushed-cotton fabric
- Paper-backed fusible webbing
- Iron and ironing board
- Scissors
- Pen
- Hot-pink sweater
- Pink, gold and turquoise sewing threads
- Scissors
- Needles: sewing, embroidery and beading
- Sewing machine
- Pins
- Gold and turquoise ribbon
- Red and black stranded cotton embroidery thread
- 3 small pink glass beads
- 1 multifaceted glass bead

HOW TO DO IT

1 Following the webbing manufacturer's instructions, iron the paper-backed fusible webbing to the reverse side of the pink cotton fabric (see page 76).

2 Draw the outline of a poodle on to the backing paper and cut it out. If you are unsure about drawing freehand, copy or trace the outline of a poodle from a picture or stencil. Remember that the poodle will be facing the opposite way from how you draw it. Here the poodle measures 9 x 10 cm (3½ x 4 in).

3 Place the sweater on the ironing board, making sure it is flat. Decide where you want the poodle to be and arrange it on the sweater until you are happy with its position. Here it has been placed in the bottom right-hand corner.

4 Remove the backing paper and iron the poodle in position by covering it with a cloth and pressing the iron on top, according to the manufacturer's instructions. Make sure you do not slide the iron back and forth over the design.

5 Stitch a decorative machine-stitch or hand-sew a blanket stitch (see page 78) around the poodle with the pink thread. For the lead (leash), pin the gold ribbon in place, from the neck of the poodle in a curved loop. Machine-stitch to secure, using a close zigzag stitch and gold thread, and turning under the short end.

6 Hand-embroider the features using a single strand of embroidery thread. Use a French knot (see page 78) in black for the eye. Use a back stitch in red for the mouth and satin or stem stitch (see page 79) in black for the feet.

7 To make the collar, pin and hand-stitch turquoise ribbon along the neck, turning under the short ends. Sew three pink beads equally spaced out on the collar using the beading needle, and making two stitches to secure each bead. Sew 1 large multifaceted glass bead to cover the join between the collar and the lead (leash).

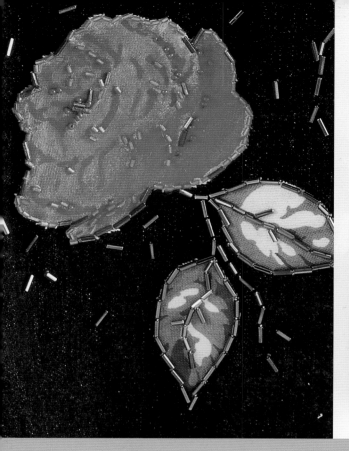

Rose Denim Skirt

APPLIQUÉD ROSES TRANSFORM a denim skirt into a work of art. Redouté-inspired splashes of full-blown blossoms are worked into a tiered design, reminiscent of a trelliswork of old-fashioned garden roses. The deep red colour stands out in sharp contrast from the dark denim background, but you can vary the effect depending on the fabric you have at hand. Pale pink flowers, for example, would work well against either a pale blue distressed denim or a pink skirt.

WHAT YOU NEED

- Floral furnishing fabric
- Paper-backed fusible webbing
- Iron and ironing board
- Embroidery scissors
- Dark denim skirt
- Red and dark red fabric paints
- Small paintbrush
- 100 red and green glass beads in various shapes
- Red and green sewing threads
- Beading needle

HOW TO DO IT

1 Following the webbing manufacturer's instructions, iron the paper-backed fusible webbing to the reverse side of the patterned fabric (see page 76).

2 Cut out the flower and leaf shapes with the embroidery scissors, cutting around and into all the detail of leaves and petals. Peel the paper backing off each shape.

3 Place the denim skirt on an ironing board and arrange the roses and leaves on the front. Iron each one in place by covering with a cloth and pressing the iron on top, according to the instructions. Work one piece at a time. Allow the skirt to cool.

4 Add extra colour to the roses with the fabric paint and a brush. Use red to intensify the colour of the roses, and highlight details in the darker red. Leave the skirt to dry overnight on a flat work surface.

5 When dry, embellish the leaves, roses and surrounding area with beadwork. Sew each bead on separately, making two stitches through each one, and knot securely on the reverse side of the skirt.

Embroidered Felt Flowers

ON HIGH-NECKED TOPS, where necklaces are difficult to wear, an embroidery-and-felt design is an accessory of its own. Knitwear, such as this lilac sweater, makes an ideal background for homespun decoration.

WHAT YOU NEED

- Cardboard and pen
- Scissors
- Pink and mauve felt
- Lilac poloneck (turtleneck)
- Strong fabric glue
- Paintbrush
- Pink, pale pink, red stranded cotton embroidery threads
- Embroidery needle
- Gold, pink and red glass beads and sequins
- Clear or coloured threads
- Beading needle

HOW TO DO IT

1 Make a cardboard template for the flower by drawing a flower shape on to the cardboard and cutting it out. Here the flower measures 3 x 3 cm (1¼ x 1¼ in).

2 Trace around the flower shape on to the felt and cut out to make one mauve and two pink flowers.

3 Place the sweater on a flat work surface. Decide on the positioning of the flowers by arranging them on the sweater. Apply a small dab of fabric glue on the reverse of each flower with a paintbrush and secure them in place. Allow to dry.

4 Use one strand of embroidery thread to stitch seed stitches (see page 78) into the centre of each flower, radiating outward . If desired, insert a piece of cardboard inside the sweater to make stitching easier.

5 Using the beading needle and clear or coloured thread, sew small glass beads at the ends of each stab stitch, making two stitches through each bead.

6 Anchor one sequin to the centre of each flower, using a bead. To do this, bring the thread through the sequin, thread on a bead, and re-enter through the same hole in the sequin, knotting the thread on the reverse side.

7 Using one strand of embroidery thread, embroider tendrils around and connecting the flower shapes, using daisychain, feather or stem stitches (see pages 78-9).

Black-Outline Flower

THE STRIKING BLACK-ON-TURQUOISE contrast enhances the pictorial quality of this flower design. Here the image was taken as an enlarged photocopy of a line drawing from a (copyright-free) flower book, but look through magazines and books for inspiration and then draw your own freehand design. For a more op-art effect, stitch overlapping concentric circles, squiggles or spirals.

WHAT YOU NEED

· Cardboard or paper and pen
· Scissors
· Turquoise sleeveless top
· Pins (for a paper template)
· 'Invisible' or 'fade away' pen fabric marker
· Thick black sewing thread
· Sewing needle

HOW TO DO IT

1 Make a template by drawing a flower shape on to paper or cardboard and cutting it out. Here a 10 x 10 cm (4 x 4 in) flower shape was used.

2 Place the top on a flat work surface and arrange the template in position on a bottom corner of the top. When you are happy with the position, trace around the template on to the top, using the pen fabric marker. If you are using a paper template, pin it in place before tracing. Remove the template and sketch in any extra detail on the flower freehand.

3 Place a piece of cardboard inside the top to separate front and back. Using thick black sewing thread and a needle, stitch over the flower outline using an even running stitch. Stitch the details within the flower.

4 To build up the design, highlight specific areas with extra stitching. Repeat a few rows of running stitch along various sections, such as on the inside of petal curves and the tips of the petals.

Pink Heart
Skirt

OVERSIZED ISOLATED MOTIFS make an impact. This Valentine-inspired heart is a stand-out-and-shout design that also gives a touch of romance to a ruffled red skirt. You can wear it girly and glamourpuss with fishnets and ankle boots or dress it down with trainers (sneakers) and a T-shirt. Choose any vibrant red-and-pink combo – try strawberry on Schiaparelli pink, vermilion on brick-red or layer the palest pastel-pink on dusky rose.

WHAT YOU NEED

- Pink satin fabric
- Paper-backed fusible webbing
- Iron and ironing board
- Pen
- Scissors
- Red cotton skirt
- Sewing machine
- Pins
- Tape measure
- Pink sewing threads

HOW TO DO IT

1 Following the webbing manufacturer's instructions, iron a length of webbing to the reverse side of the satin (see page 75).

2 Draw the heart on to the backing paper, either by tracing around a cardboard or paper template, or by folding the fabric in half and drawing half a heart along the fold line. Here a 30 cm (11¾ in) heart was used for a 50 cm (20 in) long red cotton skirt. Cut out the heart shape and peel off the backing paper.

3 Place the skirt on the ironing board and arrange the heart on the centre front, measuring to ensure it is centred and straight. Pin the heart in place.

4 Because the heart is large, you will need to work one section at a time, from top to bottom. Remove the pins for one section, cover with a cloth and press the iron on top, according to the webbing manufacturer's instructions. Repeat as necessary to fuse the whole heart in place. Allow the skirt to cool.

5 Using the pink thread, machine-stitch around the edge of the heart, using a close zigzag stitch.

An Initial 'P'

TAKING INSPIRATION from sports letters, this single letter will mark you out as an individual rather than a team member. The corduroy gives a rugged, sporty feel to the top, and the bright letter against a dark background will make you shine like a star player.

Tip

Corduroy is available in a huge range of colours, but felt or denim would give an equally rugged-looking effect. Choose fabrics that are sympathetic to your top - don't try using corduroy on lightweight cotton, for example, and avoid slippery fabrics and those that fray easily.

WHAT YOU NEED

· Yellow corduroy fabric
· Fusible webbing
· Iron and ironing board
· Cardboard or paper and pen
· Scissors
· Teal-blue sweatshirt
· Sewing machine
· Tape measure
· Yellow sewing thread

HOW TO DO IT

1 Following the webbing manufacturer's instructions, iron the webbing to the reverse side of the corduroy (see page 76).

2 Make a template by drawing a letter freehand on to cardboard, or printing out a copy of a letter in a large point size from your computer. Cut out the template.

3 Place the template the wrong way around on the reverse side of the corduroy. Trace around it on to the backing paper of the webbing, then cut out the letter.

4 Peel off the backing paper and place the letter on the centre front of the shirt. Measure to ensure that the letter is perfectly straight and centred.

5 Cover with a cloth, and press the iron on top, following the webbing manufacturer's instructions.

6 To finish, machine-stitch around the edge of the letter with yellow thread, using a close zigzag stitch.

Buttoned heart

EASIER AND LESS TIME-CONSUMING to sew on than sequins and beads are buttons. What's more, the choices are limitless: bone, shell, mother-of-pearl, brass, metal and wood are all available in a medley of colours and shapes. Use this design as a starting point: you may like to continue a line of buttons along the hem of the T-shirt, or combine large buttons with tiny ones. Smaller felt hearts in different sizes could be sewn all over, with complementary buttons on each one – some as outlines, others in the centre. Or use another shape altogether – iconographic crosses in different styles and sizes can be appliquéd on, each encrusted with embroidery, buttons and beadwork.

WHAT YOU NEED

- Light grey craft felt
- Fabric marker pen
- Cardboard
- Scissors
- Dark grey cotton T-shirt
- Tape measure
- Fabric glue (or fusible webbing)
- Paintbrush
- 20 round pink buttons
- Grey sewing threads
- Sewing needle

HOW TO DO IT

1 Using a fabric marker, draw a heart shape on the felt, either by tracing around a cardboard template, or by folding the felt in half and drawing half a heart freestyle along the foldline. Here the heart measures 8 cm (3 in) at its widest and 9 cm (3 ½ in) in height. Cut out the shape.

2 Place the T-shirt on a flat work surface and position the heart on the front centre. Measure to check that the design is centred and straight. Check that the buttons will fit around the edge so that they abut each other. If there are too few buttons, trim the heart to make it smaller and check again. Mark a guideline position for the heart with the fabric marker.

3 Use a paintbrush to spread the fabric glue evenly on one side of the heart and then press the heart in place. Alternatively, use fusible webbing (see page 75) to attach the heart.

4 Thread the needle with grey thread and sew the buttons around the heart to cover the edge. The buttons should be placed as closely together as possible, with no gaps between.

Stepping out

Mad about your Manolos? Passionate about footwear? These charming little motifs can be ironed on anywhere. Position one near the neckline, on a sleeve or pocket, or on the back of the neck to look like a new cult designer label. Or mix up a clutch of different shoe designs and iron on all over a cotton shoulderbag or the back of a jean jacket. If shoes don't excite you, there are lots of other ready-made motifs available, from floral and animal designs to more abstract shapes.

WHAT YOU NEED

- Cotton T-shirt
- Iron-on embroidered shoe motifs
- Iron and ironing board
- Pins

HOW TO DO IT

1 Lay the T-shirt flat on an ironing board and arrange the shoe motifs as desired, then pin them in place. Here one motif was placed 10 cm (4 in) from the neckline.

2 For the first one, remove the pin, cover with a cloth, and iron in place to fuse, following the manufacturer's instructions. Repeat this for the remaining motifs, and allow to cool.

Butterfly Patch Jacket

TAKE ONE DENIM JACKET AND METAMORPHOSE...

THINK WOODSTOCK with this retro hippie-style jean jacket. Adapt the glitter paint for the motif you have; you could try groovy 1960s and 1970s designs, such as a yellow smiley face, a mushroom (as sported on Kate Hudson's jeans), an ankh symbol or peace sign, or use a combination of different patches for an all-over acid-trip effect. If you like the butterfly motif, consider working repeats of the same iron-on all over the jacket, or source a really huge motif and work it on the back of the jacket, adding layers of different-coloured glitter paint for an in-your-face design.

WHAT YOU NEED

- Jean jacket
- Blue iron-on butterfly
- Iron and ironing board
- Small paintbrush
- Turquoise and blue glitter fabric paint
- Strong fabric glue
- 2 black flat-backed gemstones

HOW TO DO IT

1 Iron the embroidered butterfly motif on the top right-hand corner of the jacket by covering with a cloth and pressing the iron on top, according to the manufacturer's instructions. Leave to cool.

2 Paint glitter paint around the edge of the butterfly, and along the centre 'body' if desired, to give the motif a dash of sparkle. Leave to dry on a flat work surface.

3 Using the fabric glue, stick a black gemstone on to the end of each antenna (see page 73).

How-to Techniques

Studs and gemstones add fashionable style to jeans, jackets, handbags and T-shirts. The techniques for applying them are so easy and quick that you will have almost instant results. You can decorate a T-shirt with studs in just a few minutes' time and wear it immediately – no fuss, no waiting and no tricky materials to use. Flat-backed gemstones and diamantés in every colour under the sun can be added with just a dab of fabric glue.

INSERTING STUDS

1 Measure and mark positions for the metal studs, using a chalk or pen fabric marker. The studs look best positioned along a hem or seam and equally spaced apart.

2 Firmly press the stud into the fabric from the right side, at the desired position.

3 Turn the fabric to the reverse side and bend the prongs inward, using your thumb and fingers, a metal spoon or a screwdriver, to secure the stud in place.

ATTACHING GEMSTONES AND DIAMANTÉS

1 Dab a small amount of strong fabric glue on to the spots where you want to position the flat-backed gemstones or diamantés.

2 Pick up each gemstone, using a pair of tweezers, and position it on the glue. Allow to dry before moving the fabric.

How-to Techniques

SEQUINS ARE AVAILABLE in a huge variety of colours and forms, such as hologram dots, hearts, multicoloured discs and stars. They can be used in the same way as machine-washable glitter – to fill in a design area with sparkling colour and texture – or they can be glued on individually. Choose flat machine-washable sequins without holes for this technique, and make sure you use a generous amount of strong glue.

SEQUIN HEARTS

1 Cut out a paper or cardboard heart template, Trace around the template on to the garment using an 'invisible' fabric marker.

2 Paint a generous amount of glue inside the heart. Use a glue that is compatible with the sequins, and the same brand.

3 While the glue is still wet, liberally sprinkle the glittery heart sequins on to the glue, making sure no area of glue is left visible.

4 Press lightly down on the sequins to ensure they stick. Leave to dry until the glue has hardened, preferably overnight.

5 When dry, shake off the excess sequins on to a piece of paper to reveal the design. The surplus sequins can be reused.

How-to Techniques

IF YOU ARE USING a plain or patterned fabric, iron the fusible webbing to the entire length of the fabric; this way, you can cut out various shapes as you require them, without having to fuse more webbing on to scraps of fabric later on. The shapes you choose to draw or trace on to the paper can be as ornate or as simple as you like, but remember that you will need to machine-stitch around the edge of each appliquéd piece to prevent fraying.

WEB-FUSING THE HEART

1 Refer to the manufacturer's instructions before you begin. Iron a length of fusible webbing on to the reverse side of the fabric.

2 Cut out a paper or cardboard heart template and draw around it on to the protective paper of the webbing with a pen. Alternatively, draw a freehand image directly on to the backing paper.

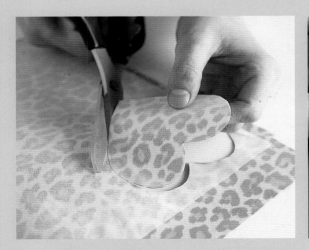

3 Cut out the heart from the fabric, using sewing scissors, following the pen outline.

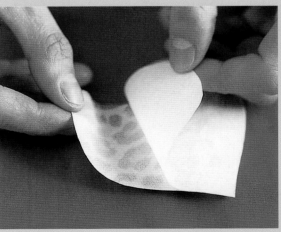

4 Peel off the protective backing paper. The appliqué is now ready to be positioned and fused in place.

How-to Techniques

CHINTZY FURNISHING FABRICS and old-fashioned prints may not look stylish or even attractive as a whole, but they can offer up some great isolated designs to use for appliqué. Search your local charity or thrift shops for fabric remnants, old clothes and curtains that have an interesting design element. The motif doesn't have to be floral; you might find yourself inspired by a boy's cowboy pyjamas, a bird or wildlife print or a simple geometric.

WEB-FUSING THE FLOWER

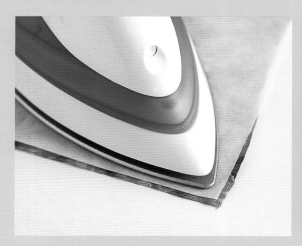

1 Refer to the manufacturer's instructions before you begin. Select the area of flower detail that you want to use and iron the fusible webbing on to the reverse side of the fabric.

2 Cut out the flower from the fabric using sewing scissors. Use embroidery scissors for cutting out shapes that have intricate, fine details or an irregular outline.

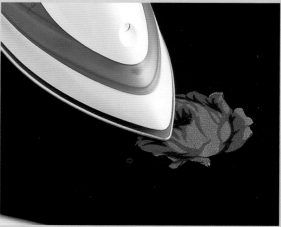

3 Peel off the protective backing paper from the fabric flower motif.

4 Position the appliqué on the garment. Following the manufacturer's instructions, fuse in place with a hot iron. Some manufacturers may recommend covering the appliqué motif with a cloth.

Glossary

TOOLS

BEADING NEEDLE
A fine needle for sewing on beads that have very small holes.

CARDBOARD
Cardboard is available in various thicknesses and qualities. Use thicker card for inserting inside clothes when painting, bleaching or printing to stop the paint or bleach going through to the other side of the fabric. Cardboard is also useful for hand-sewing, and as a substitute for a hoop for embroidery work to prevent stitching through to the other side of the article.

CHALK FABRIC MARKER
A chalk marker is useful for marking designs and measurements on to fabric, and it rubs or washes out. Some versions have a brush eraser at the end for removing the marks.

EMBROIDERY HOOP
Wooden or plastic hoops that secure fabric and keep it taut for working decorative stitches.

GLUE GUN
This electrical tool enables instant glueing and will avoid the need for pressing or clamping pieces together until they are dry. To apply the glue, insert the special glue sticks, heat up the gun and press the trigger; the glue is released through the nozzle. Although the gun cannot be used on items you want to wash, it is ideal for adding gemstones, appliqués and trims to shoes and handbags or for attaching brooch pins to fake flowers.

IRON
An iron is essential for pressing clothes and ironing on transfers and heat-fusible webbing.

INVISIBLE OR FADE-AWAY FABRIC MARKER
A special felt-tip pen used for marking fabric. The marks disappear with time.

NEEDLES
Available in a variety of sizes, specific needles are used with different types and weights of thread. Use Sharps for hand-sewing, embroidery needles for stranded embroidery thread, and tapestry needles for tapestry wool or yarn.

PAINTBRUSHES
Owning a good range of different paintbrushes will enable you to create a huge variety of effects. Use large, medium and small house-decorating brushes for creating bold splashes of colour when fabric painting or bleaching. Use fine-tipped artists' brushes for detailed work and flicking paint or bleach. Always wash brushes thoroughly after use.

PINS
Use pins for temporarily securing fabrics together, pinning up a hem or pinning on trimmings prior to sewing. Coloured-head pins are easier to see and remove than dressmaker's pins.

RULER
A transparent version allows you to see what you are measuring and enables you to line up letters or numbers horizontally. Any type of ruler is helpful when centring a design or for marking straight lines on fabric.

SCISSORS
Use sharp sewing scissors for cutting fabric and trims. Use embroidery scissors for cutting threads and trimmings, or for cutting out intricate appliqués. Use craft scissors for cutting paper or card. Do not use sewing scissors for cutting paper, as over time the blades will blunt.

SEWING MACHINE
A sewing machine enables you to create a variety of stitches, from straight and zigzag stitches to satin stitching or monogramming. Using a machine is a speedy way to attach trims and appliqués or to hem fabric.

SLEEVE BOARD
A small narrow board that clips on to an ironing board, a sleeve board is ideal for working on small areas, such as trouser legs or sleeves.

TAPE MEASURE
A flexible measuring tape that is essential for measuring fabric.

TWEEZERS
Use straight-edged cosmetic tweezers for picking up and positioning small gemstones.

MATERIALS

BEADS
Hundreds of different shapes, colours and textures of beads are available from craft shops, department stores or beading shops. Most of the beads used throughout the book are small round or straight glass beads.

BIAS BINDING
Binding is a strip of fabric cut on the bias. It is folded and pressed in such a way as to create an casing for neatly finishing the edges of fabrics and garments. You can cut your own from any fabric you like, but there are many colours and types of binding available which need only to be sewn in place.

BLEACH
This standard household fluid can be used to discolour and fade colour when it is applied on to natural fabrics and denims. Use caution when handling, as the bleach will discolour any fabric or furnishing on to which it splashes.

ELASTIC THREAD
A stretchy thread that is ideal for using on knits or stretchy fabrics, or for sewing on trim or beadwork that needs 'give'.

FABRIC GLUE
This is a special adhesive used for glueing fabric shapes, trims or gemstones on to fabric. Always make sure the glue you use is suitable for the materials. Using the same brand as the decoration will ensure the best possible adhesion. Glues specifically for use with washable glitter and sequins, and transfer foils, are available.

FABRIC PAINT
This is a special paint that can be applied on to fabric. Once fixed, usually by ironing it on the reverse side of the design, it is fully washable. Read the manufacturer's advice for fabrics to use and fixing techniques.

FEATHER TRIM
Available in various colours and styles, feather trims are secured in a simple ribbon binding for stitching on. Often feather trims include beads or a decorative trim, and can be hand-sewn on to the right side of a garment or accessory.

FELT
This is a cloth made from pressed wool. You can buy squares of craft felt in a multitude of colours from craft or specialist sewing shops. It is easy to cut and does not fray. Felted wool is a thicker more textured fabric than craft felt and can be purchased by the metre (yard) from sewing shops.

FUSIBLE WEBBING
This is a heat-reactive bonding agent that will hold an appliqué, trim or hem to fabric without stitching. It is available as a length of webbing, which needs to be inserted between two layers of fabric before ironing to fuse in place, or as a paper-backed variety, which can be fused on to one side of fabric before ironing it to the other. Read the manufacturer's recommendations for the correct fabric and the ironing technique.

GEMSTONE STUDS

These are metal clasps that have four prongs for holding gemstones. They are pressed through the wrong side of the fabric and a gemstone is inserted in the prongs. The prongs are then bent over the stone to hold it in place.

GEMSTONES OR DIAMANTES

These sparkly synthetic stones can be glued in place with fabric glue or a super glue. They can also be inserted into gemstone studs.

GLITTER FABRIC PAINT

This is a clear fabric paint containing fine glitter particles, available in a range of colours. When the paint is dry, the glitter sparkles.

IRON-ON EMBROIDERED MOTIFS OR TRANSFERS

Embroidered appliqués and pre-cut transfers have a heat-reactive webbing on the reverse side. The motifs can be positioned anywhere on a garment and ironed in place.

MACHINE-WASHABLE GLITTER

This super-fine glitter in a range of colours can only be applied to clothing with a special fabric glue made by the same company as the glitter. Read the manufacturer's instructions for application techniques.

METAL STUDS

These are available in silver and gold metal and in different shapes and sizes. They have four prongs, which are inserted through the right side of the fabric. The prongs are then opened out and pressed flat on the reverse side of the fabric to hold the stud in place.

RIBBON ROSES

These can be purchased ready-made. They can also be made by wrapping a short length of narrow ribbon into a rosette and securing the shape in place with a few stitches.

RIBBONS AND TRIMMINGS

An array of textures, colours, styles, patterns and widths are available, from velvet ribbon, sequin trim and fringing to lace, rickrack and cord. Many can be machine-stitched in place, however more delicate lace and beadwork will need to be hand-sewn.

SEQUINS

Loose sequins have tiny holes that allow them to be stitched in place individually. Sequins are also available without holes, and these are glued on with strong fabric glue. Sequin trim is a decorative length of small round sequins held together with thread, which can be hand-sewn or machine-stitched in place.

SUPER-GLUE OR CONTACT GLUE

A very strong contact glue that immediately bonds materials together. Read the manufacturer's advice for materials that can be bonded and always follow the application instructions. These types of glue should not be used on clothing.

THREADS

General-purpose cotton or polyester thread is used for hand-sewing and machine-stitching. Stranded cotton embroidery thread (floss) is used for decorative stitching; usually this is available six-stranded and the strands can be separated for finer work. Tapestry wool or yarn is much thicker than embroidery thread and is often used for embroidery work on heavier woollen garments.

TRANSFER PRINT

A coloured image is photocopied on to special transfer paper, which is then positioned on to a garment of fabric and transferred, using a special press. The technique requires enlisting the help of a specialist copier or T-shirt printing shop.

SEWING STITCHES

BLANKET STITCH

This stitch is used to hem raw edges, or as decoration. Insert the needle through the fabric so that it points up to the top edge , wind the loose thread over the needle and pull it through the loop.

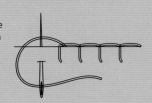

COUCH STITCH

If you are couching thread, insert it through the fabric and lay it along or round the shape. Do the same if you are couching cord, but don't insert it through the fabric. Thread another needle with a finer thread in the same or a contrasting colour, and sew even stitches across the thread/cord.

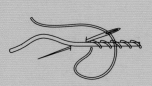

DAISYCHAIN STITCH

Bring the needle through the fabric where you want to start the chain and insert it back in just to the right of where the thread came through, to create a small loop. Insert the needle back through the fabric about a stitch length to the left and bring it up and over the looped thread. Repeat to create subsequent loops.

FEATHER STITCH

This is a decorative loop stitch that is worked alternately from right and left of a given line, following the same principles as for the daisychain stitch (see above).

FRENCH KNOT

Tie a knot at the end of the thread and insert the needle through the reverse of the fabric. Wind the thread round the needle twice and insert it back through the fabric close to where it came up.

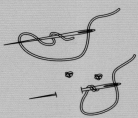

SEED STITCH

These are small, random stitches that can vary in length. Insert the needle through the reverse of the fabric and then back through at a distance to create the desired length of stitch.

Resources   Acknowledgements

SLIP STITCH

This stitch is used to hem fabric. With the needle, sew into the folded hem fabric and catch a thread from the main fabric, spacing the stitches evenly apart.

STEM STITCH

This stitch is used to outline a marked design; altering the angle of the stitch will vary the width of the stitched line. Insert the needle through the fabric and make the first stitch. Make the next stitch next door to the first, and so on, keeping the stitches even.

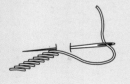

OVERHAND

These tiny, even stitches are used to join two finished edges – for example, attaching ribbon or lace edging to a garment. Insert the needle diagonally from the back edge through to the front, picking up only one or two threads each time. Insert the needle directly behind the thread from the previous stitch and bring it out a stitch length away.

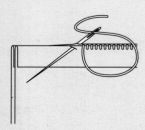

F. W. BRAMWELL & CO. LTD
Old Empress Mills
Empress Street
Colne, Lancs BB8 9HU
0123 286 0388
www.bramwellcrafts.co.uk
Glitter, foils, fabric glues and paints, gemstones and more.

DOVER BOOKSHOP
18 Earlham St
London WC2H 9LG
020 7836 2111
www.doverbooks.co.uk
Copyright-free design books.

DYLON INTERNATIONAL LTD
Worsley Bridge Rd
London SE26 5HD
Advice line: 020 8663 4296
www.dylon.co.uk
Fabric dyes, paints and pens.

ELLS & FARRIER
20 Beak Street
London W1F 9RE
020 7629 9964
www.creativebeadcraft.co.uk
Beads, gemstones, studs and trimmings.

JOHN LEWIS PLC
Oxford Street
London W1A 1EX
020 7629 7711
www.johnlewis.co.uk

The following companies were very helpful in lending props for the photography shoots:

ANDREW MARTIN (wallpapers)
200 Walton Street
London SW3 2JL
020 7225 5100

CATH KIDSTON
8 Clarendon Cross
London W11 4AP
020 7221 4000
www.cathkidston.co.uk

JACQUELINE EDGE
1 Courtnell Street
London W2 5BU
020 7229 1172
www.jacquelineedge.com

MUJI
Whiteleys Shopping Centre
London W2 4YN
Mail order: 020 7792 8283
www.muji.co.jp

THE PAINT LIBRARY
5 Elystan Street
London SW3 3NT
020 7823 7755
www.paintlibrary.co.uk

PAPERCHASE
213 Tottenham Court Road
London W1T 9PS
020 7467 6200
www.paperchase.co.uk

SANDERSONS
Sanderson House
Oxford Road
Denham, Bucks UB9 4DX
www.sanderson-online.com

I would like to thank the following designers for their customizing contributions:
Nancy Bridgewater
Katy Hackney
Claire Kitchener
Kim Robertson
Emma Eardley

Index